RACHEL CARSON

PRESERVING A SENSE OF WONDER

Fulcrum Publishing
www.fulcrum-books.com

Library of Congress Cataloguing-in-Publication Data

Locker, Thomas, 1937-
Rachel Carson : preserving a sense of wonder / by Thomas Locker and
Joseph Bruchac.
p. cm.
Summary: A biography of Rachel Carson interspersed with her own
memorable quotes.
ISBN 1-55591-482-9 (hardbound : alk. paper)
1. Carson, Rachel, 1907–1964—Juvenile literature. 2.
Biologists—United States—Juvenile literature. 3.
Environmentalists—United States—Juvenile literature. [1. Carson,
Rachel, 1907–1964. 2. Biologists. 3. Scientists. 4. Women—Biography.]
I. Bruchac, Joseph, 1942- II. Title.
QH31.C33L63 2004
333.95'16092—dc22

2003019346
2003019346

Design by Nancy Duncan-Cashman
Printed in China
0 9 8 7 6 5 4 3 2 1

Fulcrum Publishing
16100 Table Mountain Parkway, Suite 300
Golden, Colorado 80403
(800) 992-2908 • (303) 277-1623
www.fulcrum-books.com

Once there was a child whose love of nature would one day lead her to write a book that changed our world.

On a little farm not far from a bend of the
Allegheny River, Rachel saw spring fog that
seemed to turn each road into a river and the
land back into an ancient sea.

That place was called Springdale, Pennsylvania, a town once as lovely as its name. There, in a clapboard house with four small rooms, a wide-eyed girl learned from her mother, Maria, to know the names and songs of birds, and to see the spirit in all living things.

While she would not see the ocean until she was a grown woman, books began to carry Rachel away to distant shores, where the music of waves would move her heart.

Although Rachel always knew her path would
be that of a writer, she chose to study living
things—biology—in college.

When at last Rachel made her first visit to the ocean to work for one enchanted summer, her feet felt the pull of Cape Cod's salty waves, and her wondering eyes took in the great sea.

Sometimes nature lends a heart strength, and when
Rachel looked for her first job in science, her writing
saved the day. She would write radio scripts on the
romance of the waters, a subject close to her.

Later, she wrote a first book, *Under the Sea Wind*, about her great love, the wonderful sea. In its pages, Rachel followed the creatures of ocean and shore throughout the seasons.

This was only the beginning of Rachel's true stories of nature's wonders—soon she wrote *The Sea Around Us*, then *The Edge of the Sea*. Now she could write all the time and live in a cottage on the coast of Maine, where the ocean's song was always nearby.

In the Pennsylvania town where Rachel had been a

child, few trees were now left, the rivers were foul,

the air was choked with smoke, and the gentle

rain was now poisoned with sprays to kill insects.

When Rachel heard stories of robins dropping dead from eating insects treated with the chemical sprays, she could no longer be silent. She began to write a book that warned of a world where the songs of birds would disappear and the rivers and oceans would die.

Rachel's new book, *Silent Spring*, helped people understand that if we break one strand in the web of life, every other strand is in danger. While many powerful voices were raised against her, others read Rachel's words and felt their own hearts change.

Two years later, Rachel had cancer and felt her own life ending. Yet she felt peace and happiness because she knew that her books would be read by those who had never known her and that the living sea would still wash onto the shore.

Because of Rachel and her powerful words for nature, the rivers of our land now flow cleaner, the songbirds still sing from the apple trees, and the fish still swim in Rachel's beloved sea.

And like Rachel, somewhere a child watches and listens and cares for this earth as she keeps her sense of wonder.

Underlying the beauty of the spectacle there is meaning and significance. It is the elusiveness of that meaning that haunts us, that sends us again and again into the natural world where the key to the riddle is hidden.

Take time to listen and talk about the voices of earth and what they mean—the majestic voice of thunder, the winds, the sound of surf or flowing streams.

The more clearly we can focus our attention on the wonders and realities of the world about us, the less taste we shall have for destruction.

The edge of the sea is a strange and beautiful place.

Every mystery solved brings us to the threshold of a greater one.

In every outthrust headland, in every curving beach, in every grain of sand there is the story of the earth.

There is something infinitely healing in the repeated refrains of nature—the assurance that dawn comes after night, and spring after the winter.

A child's world is fresh and new and beautiful, full of wonder and excitement. It is our misfortune that for most of us that clear-eyed vision, that true instinct for what is beautiful and awe-inspiring is dimmed and even lost when we reach adulthood.

Those who contemplate the beauty of the earth find reserves of strength that will endure as long as life lasts.

If a child is to keep his inborn sense of wonder, he needs the companionship of at least one adult who can share it, rediscovering with him the joy, excitement, and mystery of the world we live in.

For the sense of smell, almost more than any other, has the power to recall memories and it is a pity that we use it so little.

The discipline of the writer is to learn to be still and listen to what his subject has to tell him.

The lasting pleasures of contact with the natural world are not reserved for scientists but are available to anyone who will place himself under the influence of earth, sea, and sky.

Rachel Louise Carson was born May 27, 1907, on a farm in Springdale, Pennsylvania. When she was ten, *St. Nicholas*, the best of all children's magazines, published her first story. She majored in biology at Pennsylvania College for Women (now Chatham College), earned a master's degree in marine zoology at John Hopkins University, and went to work for the U.S. Fish and Wildlife Service writing radio scripts. Her books include *Under the Sea Wind*, *The Sea Around Us*, and *The Edge of the Sea*. She wrote books to teach young people about nature including *Help Your Child to Wonder* and *A Sense of Wonder*. Her book *Silent Spring* was translated into more than fifteen foreign languages and has been declared the most influential book of the past fifty years. She died in April 1964 after a long fight with breast cancer.